St Swithun's Day

ST SWITHUN'S DAY

Poems from Winchester Cathedral

Stella Davis

WINCHESTER
CATHEDRAL

Some of these poems first appeared in The London Magazine, *South Poetry Magazine, and* The Spire Trust's Keeping Faith *anthology, and are reproduced by kind permission of the editors.*

...

First published by
The Friends of Winchester Cathedral

ISBN 0 903346 338

A CIP catalogue reference for this book is available
from the British Library

Illustrations courtesy of John Hardacre
Curator, Winchester Cathedral

Printed by Sarsen Press, Winchester

Cover photograph by John Hardacre

Author photograph courtesy of The Southern Daily Echo

This collection of poems resulted from my time spent as poet in residence at Winchester Cathedral in 2003. The residency was a Regional Arts Lottery Project, funded through Arts Council South East (formerly Southern Arts). Additional funding was provided by the Patrick Mace Fund, administered by the Dean and Chapter of Winchester Cathedral.

My thanks to the funding bodies, and to the Dean, Chapter, and Cathedral Community who made me so welcome.

Stella Davis, 2004

I.M. E.E.P.

1922 - 2002

CONTENTS

Part 1: The History of Footfall.

Protean.

Behind the panelling, murals.
Beyond the vaulting, blunt curves
of the Romanesque.
Under the stones, arrangements
of other stones. From the screen
a doorway. Under the grass
the shape of the Chapter House.
In the tombs, a jumble of bones.
And under the foundations,
an artesian well.

Nothing is as it seems.
The strong Cathedral calm
is no building immemorial,
but something protean, as unexpected
as the flexible hand of God.

No single route has brought us here
to this tranquil site,
only a confusion
of journeys and reverses,
a jumble of faith

and pilgrimage, and folly,
intellect, endeavour,
and endless inspiration.
Taking breath
we draw in hope, like air.

At Bishop Swithun's Shrine.

Today the ancient voices breathe only
of the sliding unreliability of matter,
scattered into dust, or at best
divided among the devout:
here a forearm, there
a stone relic, perhaps a heart.

Sainthood was never a guarantee
of reverence, and this
is Swithun so shifted:
buried, exhumed, enshrined,
made myth, broken apart,
slipping at last like vapour through
the grasp of Wriothesley,
bitter Wriothesley, blustering
over the shrine
"nothing here….no gold…..
great counterfeits…." Boasting
"At three o'clock this morning
we made an end of it."

None could destroy his glory.
Sainted, he settled stilly in
faith's obstinate mind.

Built shrines hold piety
as shallow streams hold fish,
liable to dearth and drought,
to the famous summers

that dried the mossy font
turning the water from blue
to a stretched yellow:
in history; in living memory.

And again the sun slips round,
the striping daytime lessens and lessens.
Twilight, kindly to shades,
sifts upon the site of the shrine.
Whatever partakes in God is safe in God.
Candles may, or may not, be lit.

Beyond the walls, across the grass
where the wind runs grey and restless
and the soil's life quietly takes its evening turn,
the idea of a good and modest man
that some call holy, stubbornly endures.

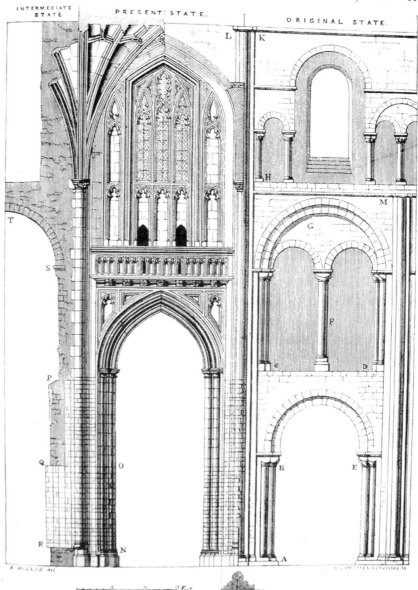

INTERMEDIATE STATE   PRESENT STATE.   ORIGINAL STATE.

The alterations to the arches of the nave

Rude Normans.

"The transepts, of a rude and plain Norman.....the oldest part of the edifice."
Revd. R. Willis, The Architectural History of Winchester Cathedral.

Certainly, they knew what they meant,
and certainly, expressed it.

Before they learnt to soar
the builders of cathedrals
threw these sturdy ladders
up to heaven:

Curve after solid curve
this wriggling vaulting,
pillar complementing pillar,
stone arching over
indefatigable stone.

Rude and plain Norman?
Yes. But it is here
in the glassy light between
these ponderous columns,
the casual believer is consoled:

For what in all of Christendom
announces quite so clearly
as the work of these
rude Normans,
that God is here to stay?

Benefactors.

Swithun

Cynegils   Cenwahl

Stigard   Alwyn

Walkelin   Waynflete

de Lucy   de Blois

Beaufort   Elphege

Wykeham   Wynford

Langton   Talbot

Fox   Edington

Poynet   Andrewes

Morley   Curle

WILLIAM ROBERT WALKER, DIVER

Bishop Beaufort's Chantry Chapel.

Bishop Beaufort started life
on the wrong side of a ducal blanket;
ended it here, in his Cardinal's hat,
enshrined below an angel, mirroring
back to him his Lancastrian arms.

An interesting journey. And after death
while his neighbour's saintly bones
were taken and dispersed, he lay
untroubled in his stone:
John of Gaunt's by-blow made good.

This is a hopeful, if worldly, story.
Some of the things that Beaufort knew
about the links that run
between piety and power,
we are less sure of now,

Being more inclined to ask
the awkward question:
Who governs? Who shall rule?
Who calls the shots?
By Whose authority?

The Tile Pavement.

Looking to heaven, the iconoclasts
missed the tile floors, as they wrought
their holy ruin, chasing after
and defeating, for the moment
idolatry and superstition
and, in their service, beauty.
                    The breaking
of the shrines and altars, the unmaking
of all the glitter afforded God
drove their harsh fists and unforgiving hearts
not once, but twice, and left
the cool and level monochrome
we now find usual.

But on the floor is something different,
unseen by high reforming minds:
only the humble worshipper,
with eyes cast down, looked under foot,
saw chequers, stars, and fleurs de lys,
saw fish and gryphons, spirals, lions,
rosettes, and leopards, and something
almost a phoenix:
the fanciful, the playful, the ornate,
the lovely and imagined: all of this
the obeisant knew was there;
said nothing
except perhaps a prayer
which kept the loving craft
of Wessex tilers
intact for us
seven hundred long, shod years.

The Restoration of the Cup to the Laity 1547.

Drink ye all of this. And so
the parched and lonely mouth
is touched communal, drouth
driven back, the lively flow
as welcome as a kiss,
as bliss, as grace:
an altering of the place
from *theirs* to *ours*, where
at the table gathering
we share
this luminous translation
For you and for many, adding
our word of celebration to
the Christian conversation of the People.

A Moment in the Garden.
Bishop Morley's Library.   For John Hardacre

I sit, for an Eden-shining moment,
out of the deep window's slant on the sun,
weeping over Paradise Lost

which lies, a first edition, in my hands
that earlier today have bagged up compost,
pricked out seedlings, scrabbled in the soil.

So unexpected is
this momentary gift
that I am not prepared. Nor is my guide
whose care the treasure is, and who
a little anguished, begs
Don't cry on the book!
I put it down, an orchid-rare
and lovely flowering,
and from a distance, wipe away
my dangerous, modern tears.

And should you ask
what moved me so
I might perhaps reply:

this seemed to me
a moment in the Garden,
and all the world, made new.

Skeptic.

Guardian Angels Chapel.

I am trying to catch
the eye of an angel
but none of them looks my way,
being blinded by time, or fixed
for ever easterly, or involved
in angelic secret-keeping smiles.

Just one of them faces outward
but even he, or is it she, or it,
has a gaze as noncommittal
as the milk-mild eye of age:
a long look from the Year of our Lord
twelve hundred and forty.

The Guardian Angels:
how coolly they stare
from the pale roof of heaven
with their mediaeval eyes.
Whom or what soever they guard,
I cannot think it is you, or me.

Sonnet for Jane Austen.

She would not like this poem: she'd maintain
I had ignored the niceties. She'd think
I was, with Mrs Elton and poor Frank,
Distinctly underbred. I'd cause her pain
For daring first to speak of her as "Jane",
And then, to mention what it was she did,
To bring out in the open what she hid
From almost everyone, and say it plain.

The two memorials are far from clear,
Alluding to the "endowments of her mind",
Or latterly, her "writings": making shift
Fastidiously, with what was left behind
By this persistent woman and her gift.
Jane wrote great novels. That is why she's here.

Broken Madonna.
Triforium Gallery.

Sweet Lady of the Fragments
innocently contained
between dismembered crowns,
there among the salvaged saints
and suzerains, kings drawn from life,
deities from the heart,

Only within her eyelids
lies the world entire:
her smile's small compass reassembles
the wreckage of our dreams.

The Marriage of Mary 1st to Philip of Spain.
Winchester Cathedral 1554.

Dealing in certainties comes Mary Tudor
to her marriage and her destiny
walking the distance of the long, long nave
all the way from heresy
to the True Faith, bedecked
and angel-headed in a veil
suffused with diamonds,
and every step a move towards
her Church restored.

The ambiguous bridegroom deals in power
and dynasty. He wonders at her age,
ponders an heir, and as she stands
dazzled beside him, smiles at England yoked,
but bears in mind the other redhead,
should this match go wrong.

Splendid, her triumph: Mary weeps
for vindication of her name, her birth,
her mother, and her faith.
Old stones stand stock. Another Church,
little and young like the dead King,
shrinks back, its agents gone to ground,
imprisoned, tortured, fled abroad,
for this is not its moment:

which yet will come, to repossess
the English route to heaven,
and mend itself from broken pieces,
many of them human.

For Winchester, no further royal weddings
will follow the misfortune of
this precedent, as misbegotten
as the veil of starry diamonds sewn
to beautify an ill-starred monarch,
masking the homely features of
a Bloody Queen.

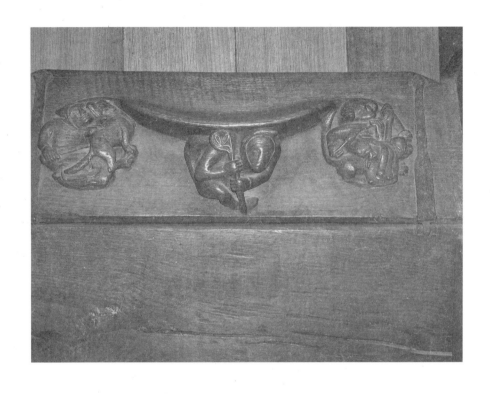

Misericord.

I'm the poor peasant props the prelate up:
a heavy load, like helping carry God.
No wonder we sometimes turn on our dogs,
or kick the cat, if one comes near. Our life
is work and sleep; and eating sometimes
(but never enough, and never very good).
The women keep at it, spinning, weaving:
they seem to know a bit better than we do
what it's all for. Inside the Church,
brightness and colour. I musn't pray
for an easier lot in life, in case
I call God's purposes in question.
So I do what I'm told. Shoulder the burden.
And take it out on the dog.

Cathedral repairs, 1673

*"To screwing a nose on the devil, putting a horn on his
head and glewing a piece on his tail, 5s 6d."*

"Some fashion the faces of angels,
or imagine Our Lord in stone,
some chisel away in good company;
I work at my task alone.
I've taken on the commission,
I'll do it the best I can,
But screwing a nose on the devil
is no sort of work for a man.

"Some carve from the face of nature,
with flowers and leaves and a snail,
but I am dealing with horns and hooves
and a diabolical tail.
I suppose my contribution
must be part of God's plan,
But screwing a nose on the devil
is no sort of work for a man.

"Some work on the Resurrection,
and some on the Holy Ghost,
some clean up the Virgin Mary,
or re-gild the heavenly host.
I envy their preoccupations,
the whole of the scriptural clan,
Because screwing a nose on the devil
is no sort of work for a man."

South Presbytery Aisle.

From here it has the look
of something on the slide,
of vast solidity
listing into decline, inexorably
as the faltering light of day.

Float a belief on water,
lash it to rafts that rot,
dive for it, salvage it, stem
disintegration, prop
the lovely thing that towers
in the mind's eye.

Vertiginous faith:
tilted, for ever frozen
in the act of falling.

Cryptic: A Seasonal Play for Several Voices.

Spring:
..And of course you must visit the Crypt. It stretches under the whole of the eastern end. You haven't really seen the Cathedral, until you've seen the Crypt.

May I visit the Crypt?
Oh no. The Crypt floods in winter. The Crypt is under water. You're not allowed in the Crypt.
I could put on my wellies.......
NO.

Summer:
...And of course you must also see the Crypt. It is amazing. We must fix a date for that.

Which day shall I come, to visit the Crypt?
(silence)
Hello? I can come any day, to visit the Crypt....?
(silence)

The Crypt is dry now: might I
visit the Crypt?
The Crypt is not open to the public.

But I am not the public, I am the poet
in residence.
Not in the Crypt you're not.

Autumn:
...And get one of the virgers to show you the Crypt.
They often go in the Crypt; you could go too.

Would you arrange for me to visit the Crypt? I should like
to see it, before the rains begin.
There is a problem....

Winter:
Before I leave, do you think
I could visit the Crypt?
Oh no, the Crypt floods in winter:
You're not allowed in the Crypt.

The History of Footfall.

All morning I have been wandering among tombs
hoping the dead in their marble cocoons might speak out
in the cause of faith and footsteps, footsteps and faith.

I never thought to encourage ghosts
nor imagined the contemporary moment
so active with shades. Something in stone
absorbs the history of footfall,
quiet on the south aisle,
steady in the nave,
processional from the transept:
footprint on footprint

back and back, through ceremonial, towards
the age when to have trust in God
or fear of God, was usual, was
a probable condition.

The sift of centuries
has riddled faith. Maybe
we substitute now the soft
shoe shuffle of carelessness
for the terror of the tramp
towards hellfire,

but keeping a foothold
we tread the same tiles,
breathe the same invocation.
                    The ghosts
have no trouble
in recognising us.
Their whispers haunt our prayers.

Stand here for the present:
this is the place; this time
the time is now.

Part II: St Swithun's and Other Days.

Advent.

The rain clears early and cold
so that crossing the Close
we catch the thin white shimmer
of winter sunshine.

Woodsmoke and bells
lift together, a chorus of rightness:
Whatever it is that begins,
begins here.

Quickening, we embark
on the exploration, plunge
through complicated paths to a simple start
and a difficult conclusion,

And bright for a moment
in the dark days of winter
the Church's year declares itself:
renewable as daybreak.

Drunk at the Back.
(*Christmas Eve 2000*)

There's a drunk at the back,
calling out as the voices lift
rumbling his raucous notes against
the soar of the sound:

angels, we sing of, *touching harps*,
and the choir's note seems to rise
the whole height of the nave;
and there's a drunk at the back
not listening as we sing *Oh*
hush your noise, ye men of strife,
And the sidesmen come, discreet,
a presence, dark-coated, firm,
and *hear the angels sing*
as might be possible, they might
be angel voices, clear, high,
floating, meantime,
Beneath the angel strains have rolled
And the notes roll down the columns
Two thousand years
and drunk at the back
our man of strife rolls down
to a fitful grumble,
and the carol dies down
and there's a rustling, a kneeling,
or mostly a Protestant squat
as shuffling and coughing
gloved hands clasped we pray

for *peace on earth*
or perhaps just peace of the heart
for the *age of gold*, or just
for one golden night
this night
as the lights glow
and midnight is near
and the air is suffused
with possibility
and the drunk at the back
is the first to say:
A merry, merry Christmas.
And so it is.

Study of a Canon.

Books are ubiquitous, familiar:
Morris; Bonhoeffer; Tennyson;
Gombrich; St Augustine; Jung;
the shelves dipping and bulging,
the accretion endless, diffuse.

By contrast monolithic, sculptures
demonstrate their single purpose:
Remember the truths
of the Crucifixion
are harsh.

The wide window casts
an elegant eye across
the Cathedral's southern flank.
Pale winter sunlight slips
slantwise over a fine old rug:
the middle morning
merges to afternoon.

The tall chair swivels, creaks, windmilled
by long restless limbs. He doesn't say
cathedral days are running out for him,
that he'll be gone by Whit,

his legacy the stern metallic
Christ of the uncompromising eye.

Spring Cleaning.

Not quite spring, and across the emptied nave
moves a mechanical device
of considerable age
and Heath Robinson design:
the virgers are swabbing the floor.
The wet flags shine.

Scent of lilies softens the cold air.
Few but dedicated, visitors
(men in long coats, and women
in warm, but by no means knitted, hats,
and decorative boots) step delicately
over the dowsed stone,

Where the virgers can be seen
working slowly east,
tangling with handles and trailing wires,
young and quietly laughing, their robes
determinedly swishing, swishing,
swishing the spring clean.

Cycling to St Cross.

Playing hookey on a perfect spring morning,
March, but so mimicking May
that the still-bare trees startle, incongruous,
I am off along a track
battered with use to all-year dust
or mud, although
no over-walking can diminish
the stream it runs beside,

Which is all clarity and coots
and yellow wagtails,
silky emerald drownings,
and flickering fish among
clean reedy gleams, a heaven
spilt out in water. Famously
Keats came this way:
well, lucky Keats. And here
was settled down a benefaction
in the water-meadows,
grave grey stone
out of the sparkling source.

Old foundations weather well
in this kind climate, even when
we do our best to silt the air
with the detritus of
our restless journeyings.

Proper today, to move between
these venerable buildings
quietly, and hear the river's
rilling babble, as it sounded
to poets and to pilgrims both,
Henry de Blois, and Johnny Keats,
Miss Austen careful of her shoes,
whole litanies of clergy, and
the flow of those who follow in
their splendid footsteps.
Lucky too, I turn the bike,
head back to work. It's spring:
the year spins, easy as a wheel.

On the day of the invasion.

It gets us nowhere, and of course
it altered nothing. Nevertheless
I find I cannot leave unrecorded
the boy with the long hair
who sat in the Close
on the day of the invasion

playing his guitar, and singing
Masters of War, again and again
as Evensong ended
and light sank down
and the city and I
went home.

Easter Day.
Sursum Cordae

This is the day
for the lifting up of hearts
which too often lie heavy
in the breast, or pump
so fast that all momentum
is used for surging on;
or just tick over, not wanting
to be disturbed,
as the world and its demands
dictate the pulse,
and capacity for wonder
sickens a little more
with every year.

But this is our holiday
from human necessity:
a day to risk
the flight of the heart.

Whitsun Bells.

Sounding, changing
summer morning
sweet and certain
Pentecost bells

Grandsire Doubles
Double Oxford
London, Bristol, Pudsey Surprise

Lifting, waking
Sunday morning
through the city
clangs and calls

Grandsire Doubles
Double Oxford
Plain Bob, Little Bob, Bristol Surprise

Rounding, chiming
Whitsun morning
the singing spirit
springs and wells

Grandsire Doubles
Double Oxford
Stedman, Winchester Surprise.

Schools' Week.

Midsummer Day, and the Inner Close
is sprouting children all about
the carefully-tended green:
the primary colours of this
Diocesan day out,

all the Jacks and Matts and Chloes,
the Debbies and Katies and Dans,
unpeeling their lunches, behind them
a morning hazy with history,
handiwork, pilgrims, pens,

and waiting for them, the journey home,
the inevitable essay-brief
What I did at the Cathedral;
Then the end of junior school;
summer; the future; life.

Common Worship.

They've changed the words again. These forty years
have breached the bounds that held
the spoken English Church.

Almighty and most merciful Father
we have erred and strayed from thy ways like lost sheep

Miraculously, the language-fabric stands,
though blotched and full of gaping holes,
botched with verbal breeze-blocks

Forgive us our trespasses
as we forgive them that trespass against us

its pock-marked walls propped up
by makeshift girders, pvc windows
glaring like angry eyes

We acknowledge and bewail our manifold sins and wickedness

And now comes Common Worship, not altogether shoddy,
puts back old stones, flanks the façade
with broken bits of carving

Cleanse the thoughts of our hearts by the inspiration of your holy spirit

And under the stone-cladding lie
the unfatigued foundations. So
may the uncommon worshipper

not weighing our merits, but pardoning our offences

once in a way, stumble upon a marvel:
some soaring vocables, a flight
from stone to sky

Heaven and earth are full of thy glory,
Glory be to thee, O Lord most High

And stand in wonder at
a miracle configured,
seeing through mutilated doors

The peace of God, which passeth all understanding

a lovely living structure:
may yet step in, become a part
of every treasured, every measured, word.

Red Currants.

After my tour of the tower, I sit
eating red currants in the shade.

The small fruits shine and glow
like polished stones,
bite ripe and sharp, the juice
of summer's sweet
and fiery essence
tanging my tongue.

I eat them slowly
telling happiness
bead by perfect bead.

St Swithun's Day.
"that the sweet rain of heaven may fall upon my grave." Attr. St Swithun.

As words at noon from the high silt of summer
whisper of sweet pools, of limbs in a cool stream,
as rumours of flooded meadows
spread among dry pavements
and down in the damp crypt
watery recognitions ripple and surge

As the great church lies galleon-like at anchor
resting on welling life, so, stirred by the season,
disembodied the gentle ghost of Swithun
across the parched Close longingly ranges

And the child cries, and the old man grumbles,
and the organ-peal is a drift of thunder;
and youths and stout matrons collide in doorways,
and lovers catch cloudscapes in each other's eyes,
and a white lick of lightning slices dust from weary trees,
and prelates wonder in arid arches

Then every ordinary progress leads
from the ordered life to another world outside,
to a sudden unburdened flagrant openness

that the sweet rain of heaven may fall upon us all.

Acknowledgements.

I am very grateful to all of those I encountered in the Cathedral Community, clergy, staff and volunteers, who helped me to make the most of this residency. My particular thanks go to Dean Michael Till and Canon Keith Walker, to Simon Barwood, Peter Bennett, Cheryl Bryan, Sandy Davis, Chris Durant, Alison Kemp, Kathyn Vere; to Daren Gibb, and everyone at the virgers' vestry; to James Harris and Charles Lidbury each of whom helped poems to occur; to Ron James, representing the Patrick Mace Fund, for his stalwart backing; to my fellow-poets who took part in the readings and otherwise encouraged me, especially Canon David Scott and Wendy Cope; to Professor Michael Wheeler; to Janet Green and Julian Harvey of the Friends for help with this publication; to John Hardacre for contributing his time and expertise to provide the book with its illustrations, as well as for poetic inspiration in the Library; and most particularly to Keiren Phelan, Literature Officer Arts Council SE, and Canon Flora Winfield, whose unstintingly enthusiastic support has been invaluable.